Rita
THE SHAWSHANK DOG

Written and Illustrated
by
Brad Mavis

For my parents...

Foreword
by
Jodiviah Stepp

This is a story for those who love dogs and for those who love the film, "The Shawshank Redemption."

Rita's story, in part, is shared by countless other animals, that for whatever reason, find themselves alone.

It is my greatest hope, that by sharing Rita's experience, some people will be inspired to open their hearts and homes to animals in need.

"Until one has loved an animal, one's soul remains unawakened."

- Anatole France

On June 13, 1993, filming began on "The Shawshank Redemption" at the abandoned prison known as the old Reformatory in Mansfield, Ohio.

What follows is the true story of Jodiviah Stepp and Rita, the Shawshank Dog.

"Rita Hayworth and the Shawshank Redemption," a short story by Stephen King, is about survival, friendship, and escape.

I became part of a film based on that story never knowing that, at the same time, I would have my own experience that possessed those very same themes.

After an audition with other local talent, I was selected to be one of the new convicts who comes to Shawshank prison with the Tim Robbins character, Andy Dufresne. The night before filming began, I was so excited, I never slept.

My first scene is on the vintage bus.

'New Fish' convicts before wardrobe. Jodiviah Stepp is center with the blue hat.

The prison was surrounded by a high wall, and the inside was like another world. There were famous people, abandoned buildings converted into movie sets, and hundreds of extras dressed as prisoners and guards.

Electricity filled the air. There was an excitement and a heart pounding anticipation that something magical was about to happen.

It was lights, camera, action, and everything Hollywood was supposed to be.

Tim Robbins and Jodiviah Stepp preparing to film a scene.
(Photo courtesy of the Galion Inquirer).

Many of the significant prison yard scenes, such as the cons running up to the bus, Andy and Red playing catch, hundreds of prisoners being serenaded with music, or Andy dumping pieces of his cell wall from his pocket, were all shot those first two weeks.

It was about that time that we heard about the dogs.

Two strays that called the prison home had almost wandered into a scene being filmed. There was concern that they could have been hiding in the background, maybe even unnoticed when some of the other scenes had been filmed.

The word went out to round them up, but there were too many hiding places in that old prison, and the dogs knew them all.

They got the message, though...no dogs allowed in the film! After that, they seemed content to watch us from a distance in the shade of that high wall. When we didn't see them, I'm sure they were watching from one of their favorite hiding spots. I suspect that when we had all gone home each night, and the prison was once again theirs, they would venture out, hoping to find a scrap of food left behind.

By mid-July, nearly half of the film was completed. It was soon after, rumors began. Word got around that the dogs might be mean. Somebody had gotten close, and the smaller one had shown its teeth before running away.

Nobody wanted to get near them after that...

Someone once told me that, in life, you don't always choose special moments; sometimes they choose you.

Maybe I never really understood what that meant until one hot July day when I decided to take my lunch break in the shadow of that prison wall.

I had just sat down when I saw the dogs. We'd never been this close.
They were hiding in a patch of weeds at the base of the wall, curled up
against the cool stone.

I'd been around dogs my entire life and had never seen two who looked
more sad or alone. They had a thrown-away look, dirty and abandoned,
like the prison. I held out some food, but they never moved a muscle.
They just sat, looking puzzled, as if they had never known a moment of
kindness.

I broke off some of my sandwich and threw the pieces close to them. Unable to resist this temptation, they cautiously emerged.

They ate slowly, savoring each bite, as if the taste were a dream, and, if they ate too quickly, the dream would be over. Before I knew it, I had fed them my entire lunch, all but a doughnut that I had brought for my dessert.

They had already started moving on to the next hiding spot when I called out to them. The larger dog kept moving, but the little brown dog stopped and looked back.

I held up the doughnut. I was surprised when she began timidly to return to me.

She kept her head down, too shy to look at me. Every few steps, she paused as if she might change her mind and run back to her friend. I think finding the trust for the last few feet was the hardest for her. So hard that, in some submissive gesture, she crawled the rest of the way. Slowly she raised her head, and that's when I saw those teeth. I remembered the vicious dog rumors, and hoped she would just take the doughnut and not my fingers.

Ever so gently, she ate from my hand. As she did, I slowly reached out to pet her head. There was nothing vicious about her. Those teeth were not a threat but more a crooked smile caused by an underbite. Maybe she returned because she was braver than her friend. Perhaps she was just still hungry. I like to think that she was able to sense that she could trust me.

So that's how a friendship began, on that hot July day, between an actor and a stray dog finding trust over a piece of pastry. As I watched her return to her friend, I felt special, and I think I made her feel like a real dog, even if it were for just a moment.

After that, I tried to find the dogs every day. I took them something to eat and something cool to drink. Day by day, I began to notice a difference. Their timid ways began to fade, and when they approached me, there was a confidence in their walk. Sometimes when I looked for them, they were already there waiting for me.

Although the larger dog remained shy, the little brown dog seemed to want to bond with me. She no longer carried her head down. Instead, she gazed at me with eyes that seemed to communicate a humble gratitude. Something began to change for me, too. My time spent with them began to feel more like a promise that I would always be there for them. My impulse to take them home was halted only because I lived in an apartment building that did not allow pets. I decided, though, if I could not give them a home, I would find somebody who could.

I began asking everyone I knew, but finding a home for two rag-tag strays was not as easy as I'd hoped. No one wanted them. By mid-August, my inquiries were turned down with such frequency that I would expect to hear "no" before I even finished asking the question.

Things grew worse when the news was released that most of the prison would be torn down when filming was complete. The dogs would have nowhere to go. Before the final day of filming, I lay awake in bed, thinking of them. They had stirred within me a sympathy that I could not escape, and I admitted to myself what the truth had been all along. The summer had been as much about the dogs as it had been about the film, and I could not leave them behind. I then decided that I would try to hide them in my apartment just until I could find them a home.

On my last day of filming, I arrived early. I went to find the dogs, but they weren't in any of their usual spots. Somehow I knew they were gone. I could sense they were survivors and no doubt instinct had told them it was time to move on.

In the end, I had nothing more for them but a vague vision of seeing them safe and happy in a home with a big backyard. I wished I could see them just one more time, especially the little brown dog. That's when I realized I'd never even given them names.

We completed the scenes that day, and the director yelled, "Cut!" The best summer of my life was over. As I made my way back to the wardrobe trailer to change out of my prison costume, a production assistant found me and said that I was wanted back on the set.

When I arrived, the director, Frank Darabont, was waiting. He was holding a leash, and at the end of that leash was a dog that I did not recognize. It had short, shiny brown fur and wore a bright red collar. Not until the dog looked up and showed me that toothy smile did I realize who it was...

It was the little brown dog.

The director said that he had seen me with the dogs, and not wanting to leave them behind, he had some of the film crew coax them in with food. He had the dogs checked by a vet before sending them to a groomer.

Darabont had named the dogs Rita and Hayworth from the King story, "Rita Hayworth and the Shawshank Redemption," on which the film was based.

Hayworth had found a home, but Rita was saved for me.

"I'd noticed that this dog seemed to really like you," he said. "I was hoping that you might want to give her a home."

I quickly said, "Yes!"

Turning to leave, I looked down at Rita by my side, and as she looked up at me, I was reminded once again that sometimes special moments choose you.

I wish I could say that it was easy in the beginning...

I wish I could say that she was happy in her new home with me...

I wish I could say these things...

I think it was hard for her to get accustomed to life inside. She spent her days staring out the window, lost in thoughts of someplace else. At night, she hid under my bed and had trouble sleeping.

We went for walks in a nearby park, and when she saw another dog, she would become excited, and wag her tail. I think she always hoped it was her friend, Hayworth, but of course, it never was. She seemed to have been happier at the prison with her friend.

During her unhappiest times, she would scratch and chew on herself. I thought she had allergies, and I tried giving her baths with medicated shampoos.

Her symptoms, though, were caused by a condition the vet called separation anxiety. I had returned to college, and when I was in classes, she struggled with being alone.

She had to wear a cone around her neck so that she didn't scratch her face. No matter what I did, I was unable to reach her as I had at the prison. It seemed as if our one-time bond were lost.

That's why I will never forget the night that all of that changed. An approaching storm awakened me. From my bed, I could see Rita shivering in the corner, frightened by the thunder and lightning. I pulled back the covers. "Come on, Rita," I said. "Come up here with me." There was another flash of lightning, and in one quick leap, she was beside me.

The next night there was no storm, but when I came into my room, Rita was waiting on my bed. She slept with me every night after that.

Day by day, she became that friendly little dog I had once known.

When Rita met new people, I would tell them that she had once been a stray living in an abandoned prison, that she had almost been a movie star, and how she had gotten her name. The story endeared her to many, and she began to be known as the Shawshank Dog.

It's amazing what love and a home can do for an animal that has known neither. They sense what you've done for them and thank you every day by becoming your 'always dog.'

Always there to greet you when you return home.

Always by your side.

Always there when no one else is.

A year later I graduated from college and having never been caught by my landlord, we moved from that apartment into a house with a big backyard.

The new yard was surrounded by a tall fence. I think that the fence reminded Rita of the prison wall where we first met. When she sat in the shade of the fence, perhaps she felt a little more at home.

For nine years, we shared a rare bond. She was my friend, and I was hers.

"...hope is a good thing, maybe the best of things, and no good thing ever dies..."

- Andy Dufresne, "The Shawshank Redemption"

Rita died on September 9, 2002, after a long illness. She was in my arms.

I miss her and that crooked smile every day. She was a good thing, and as the movie says, "No good thing ever dies."

Though Rita could never be replaced, I could do something meaningful because of her. I could offer hope to another dog.

A few days after her death, I visited a local animal shelter and adopted a two-year-old Irish setter mix named Abby. She was big and clumsy but had the heart of a clown, able to make me laugh even at my lowest moments.

Now, years later, she is my 'always dog,' the one who sleeps beside me every night.

Without Rita, I would never have known Abby, and Abby may never have known hope and a home.

Andy Dufresne said that hope may be the best of things.

Rita showed me many things, such as love, loyalty and friendship. But I will always most appreciate what more she showed me about "the best of things..."

Now I know,

"the best of things" aren't always the prettiest...

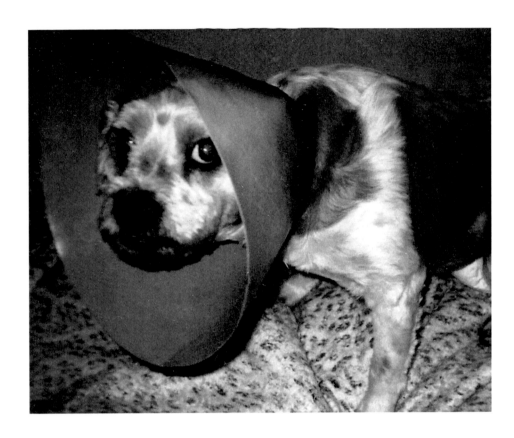

"The best of things" aren't always the easiest...

And sometimes when you least expect it, the very best of things can happen.

So...the next time you are watching "The Shawshank Redemption," think of Rita and look very closely.

Maybe, just maybe, hiding somewhere in the background, you might catch a glimpse of my little Shawshank Dog.

Some, who met Rita and learned of her story, were inspired to adopt their own "Shawshank" dog. The following pictures are of just some of the homeless dogs who found hope because of Rita.

Molly

Katie

Nino

Chief

Jewel

Toby

If you are looking for a friend, visit your local animal shelter. Perhaps a "Shawshank" dog is waiting for you.

Brad Mavis is a graduate of the
Columbus College of Art and Design.
He currently lives in Ohio with his dog Molly.

Other books by this author are available
on Amazon and barnesandnoble.com.

Rita the Shawshank Dog

A portion of the sales from each book will go
to causes that aid homeless and abused animals.

Go to Rita the Shawshank Dog's Facebook
page and share a story about your pet.

Visit Rita's website at www.shawshankdog.com.

Made in the USA
San Bernardino, CA
31 August 2019